PIANO SOLO

THE CLASSICAL WEDDING

ISBN 978-0-634-02597-6

7777 W. BLUEMOUND RD. P.O. BOX 13819 MILWAUKEE, WI 53213

Visit Hal Leonard Online at
www.halleonard.com

CONTENTS

Adagio cantabile
Second Movement from Piano Sonata in C Minor, Op.13

Ludwig van Beethoven
1770–1827

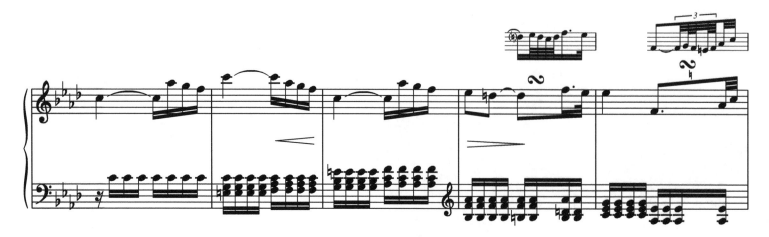

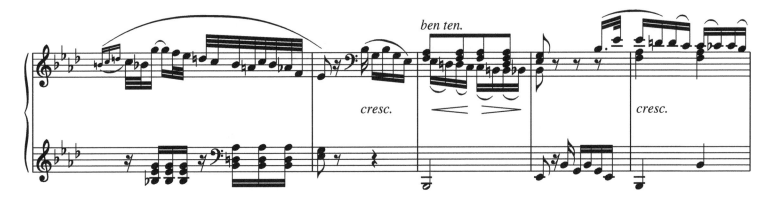

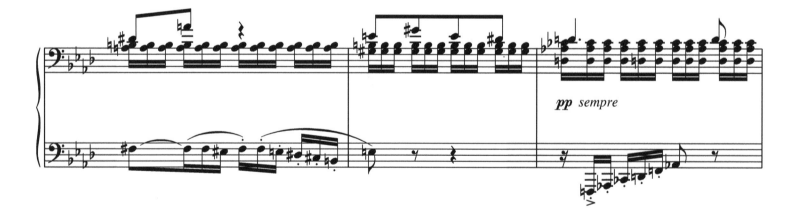

Adagio in G Minor

Tomaso Albinoni
1671–1751
originally for organ and strings

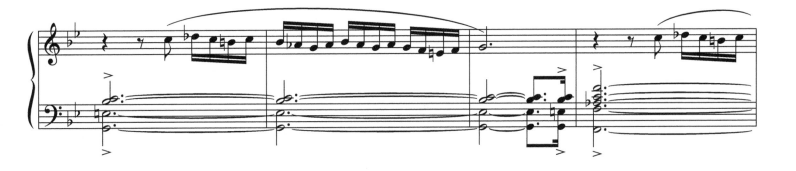

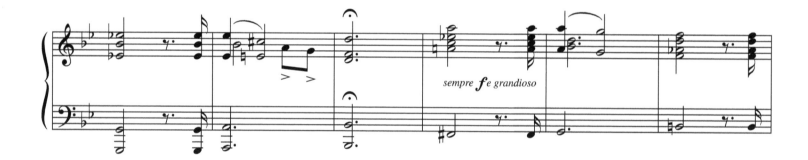

Allegro
from WATER MUSIC

George Frideric Handel
1685–1759
originally for orchestra

Air
from WATER MUSIC

George Frideric Handel
1685–1759
originally for orchestra

Andante con moto

Air on the G String

from ORCHESTRAL SUITE NO. 3 IN D

Johann Sebastian Bach
1685–1750
BWV 1068
originally for orchestra

Adagio

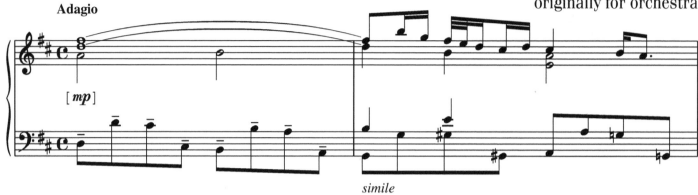

[mp]

simile

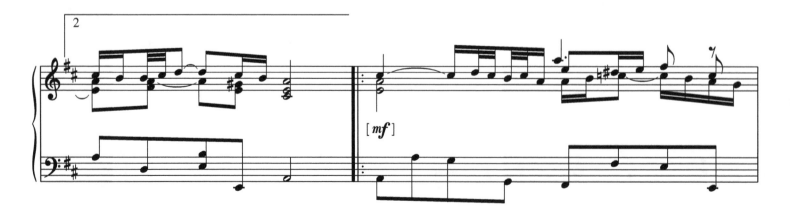

[mf]

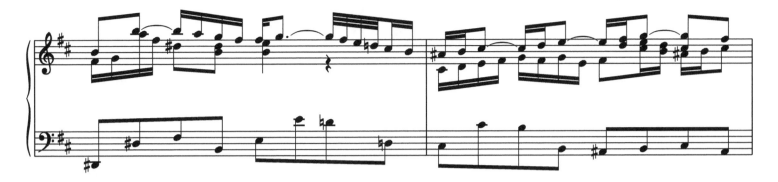

Allegro maestoso
from WATER MUSIC

George Frideric Handel
1685–1759
originally for orchestra

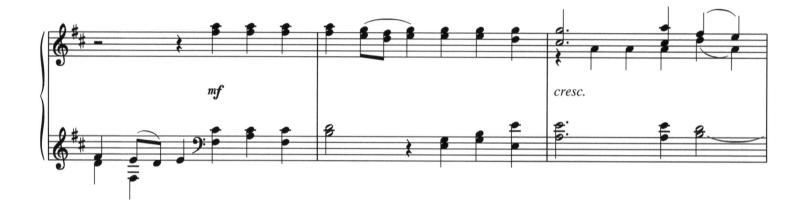

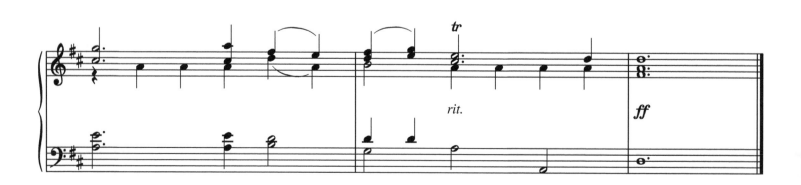

Ave Maria
based on Prelude in C Major by J.S. Bach

Charles Gounod
1818-1893
originally for chamber ensemble

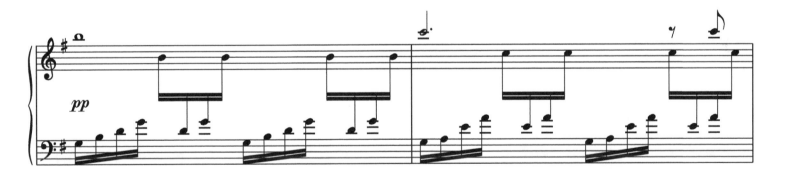

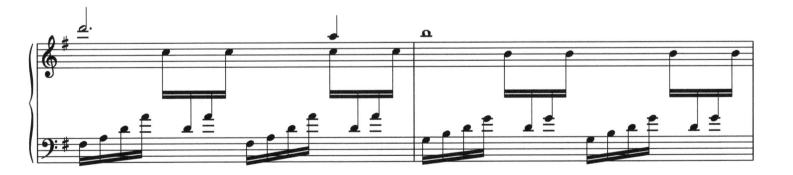

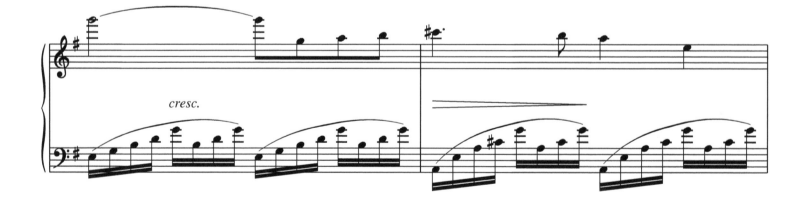

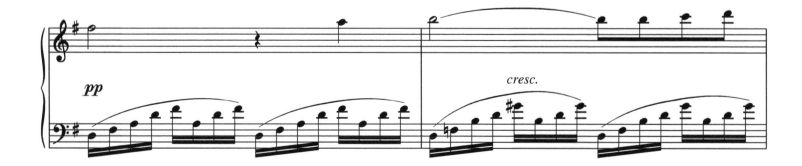

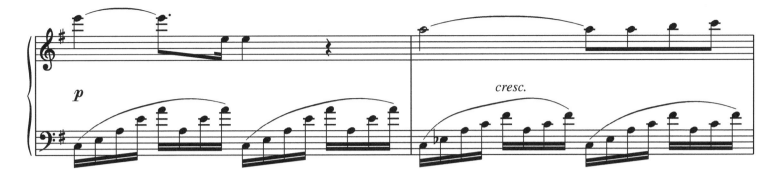

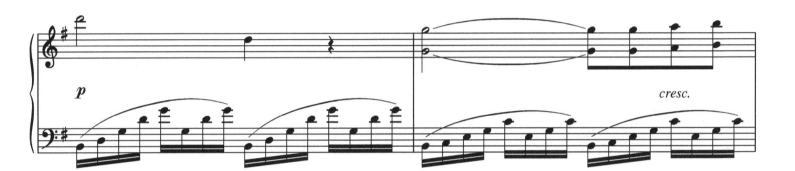

Alleluia
from the solo motet EXSULTATE, JUBILATE
Excerpt

Wolfgang Amadeus Mozart
1756–1791
K 165
originally for soprano and orchestra

Allegro non troppo

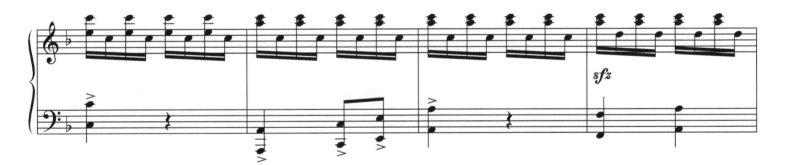

Autumn
from THE FOUR SEASONS
First Movement Excerpt

Antonio Vivaldi
1678–1741
Op. 8, No. 3
originally for violin and orchestra

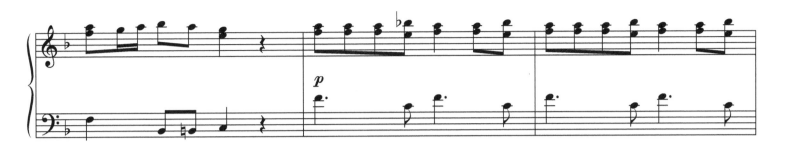

Ave Maria

Franz Schubert
1797–1828
D. 839
originally for voice and piano

Molto lento

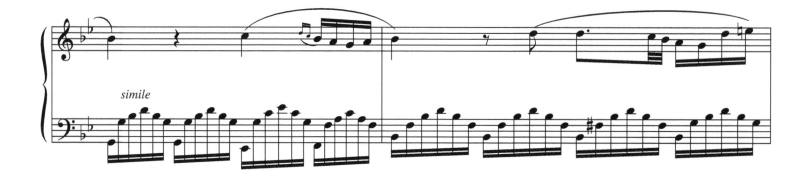

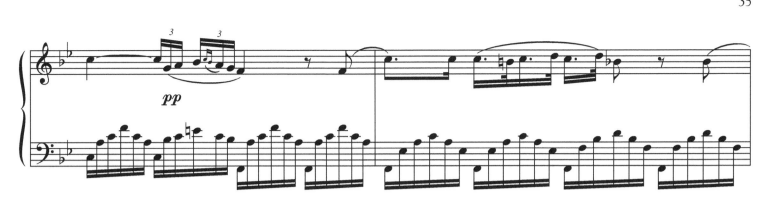

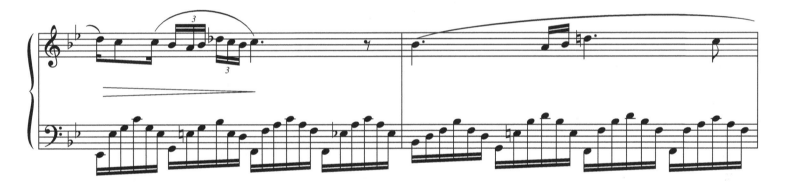

Ave verum corpus

Wolfgang Amadeus Mozart
1756–1791
K 618
originally for chorus and orchestra

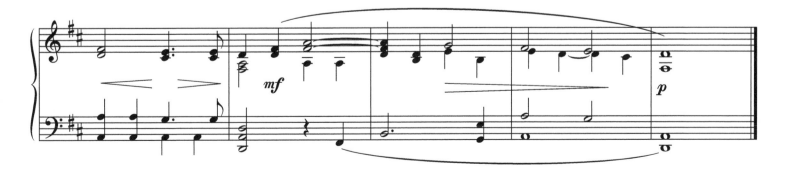

Bist du bei mir
(Be Thou with Me)

Johann Sebastian Bach
1685–1750
BWV 508
originally for voice and figured bass

Bridal Chorus
from the opera LOHENGRIN

Richard Wagner
1813–1883

Canon in D Major

Johann Pachelbel
1653–1706
originally for 3 violins and continuo

Adagio

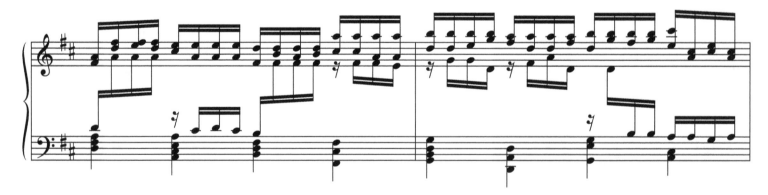

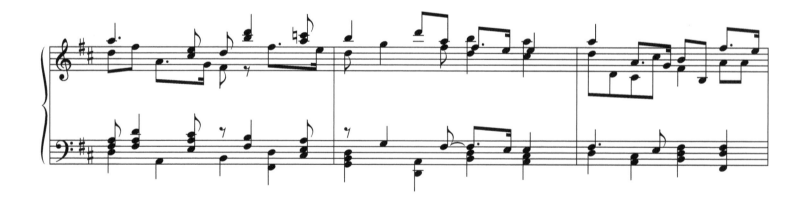

Hallelujah
from MESSIAH

George Frideric Handel
1685–1759
originally for chorus and orchestra

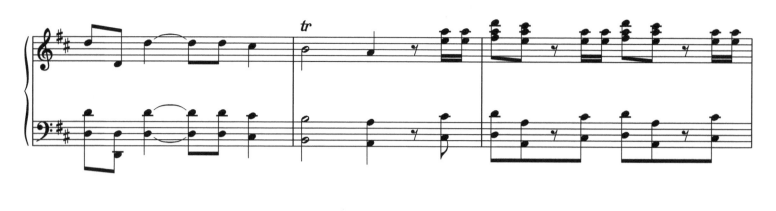

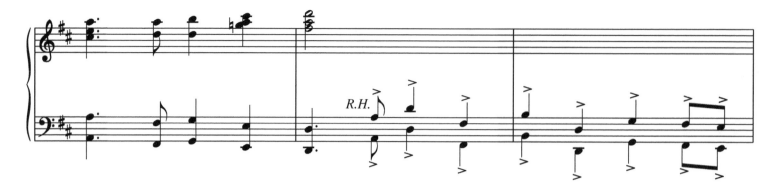

Gloria in excelsis
from the Mass GLORIA

Antonio Vivaldi
1678–1741
originally for chorus and orchestra

Allegro

Eine kleine Nachtmusik

(A Little Night Music)
First Movement Excerpt, "Serenade"

Wolfgang Amadeus Mozart
1756–1791
K 525
originally for string ensemble

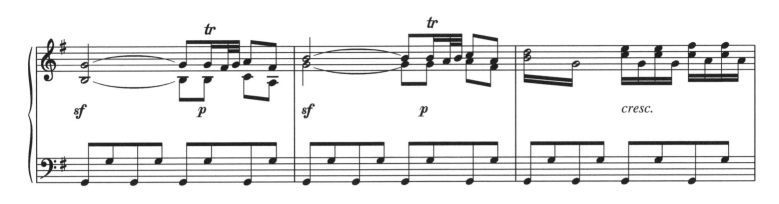

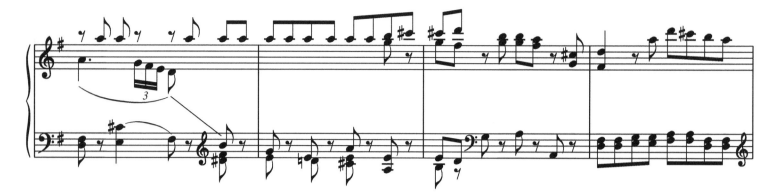

Eine kleine Nachtmusik

(A Little Night Music)
Second Movement Excerpt, "Romanza"

Wolfgang Amadeus Mozart
1756–1791
K 525
originally for string ensemble

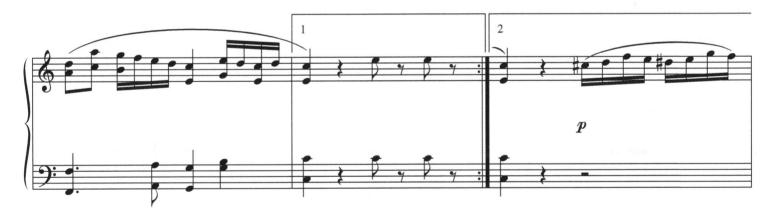

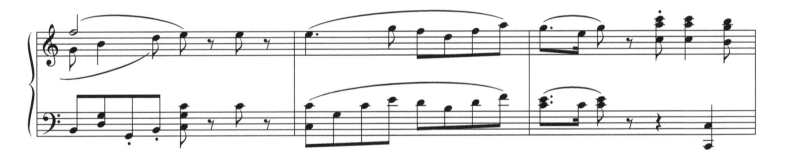

Eine kleine Nachtmusik
(A Little Night Music)
Third Movement Excerpt, "Minuet"

Wolfgang Amadeus Mozart
1756–1791
K 525
originally for string ensemble

Allegretto

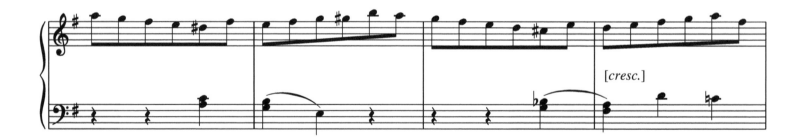

D.C. al Fine

Eine kleine Nachtmusik

(A Little Night Music)
Fourth Movement Excerpt, "Rondo"

Wolfgang Amadeus Mozart
1756–1791
K 525
originally for string ensemble

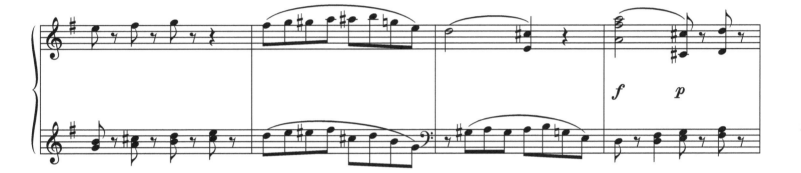

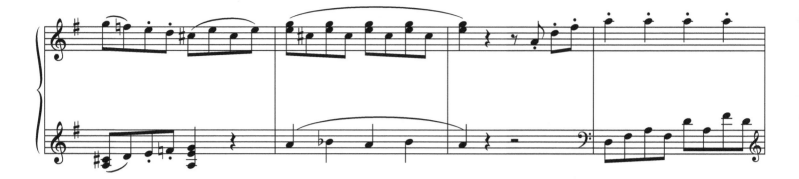

Jesu, Joy of Man's Desiring

Jesus bleibet meine Freude

from CANTATA 147, HERZ UND MUND UND TAT UND LEBEN

Johann Sebastian Bach
1685–1750
BWV 147
originally for choir and orchestra

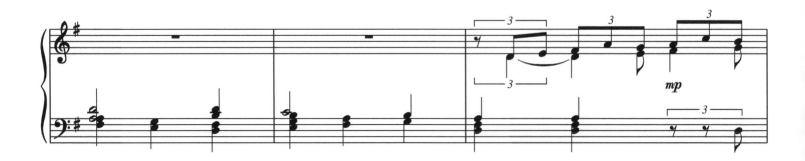

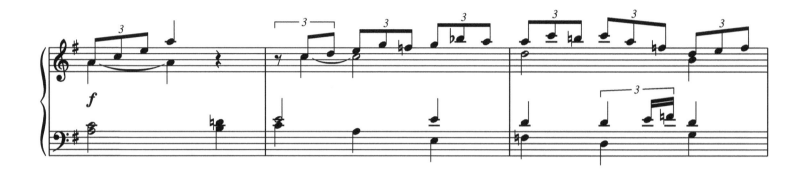

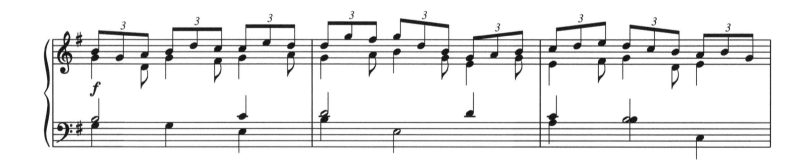

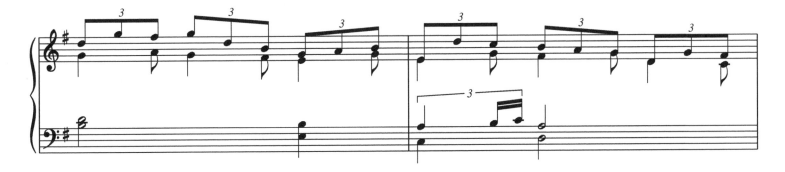

Intermezzo in A Major

Johannes Brahms
1833–1897
Op. 118, No. 2

Andante teneramente

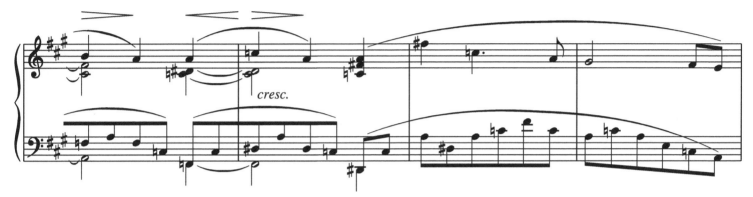

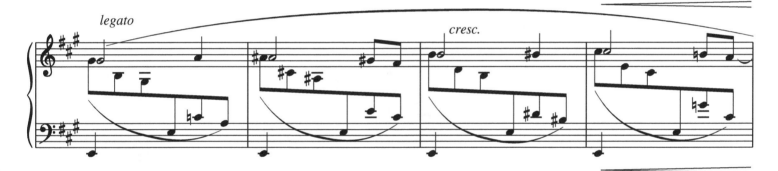

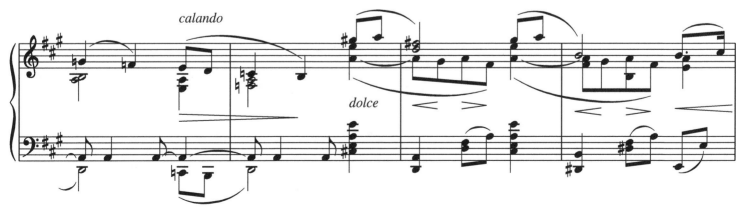

cresc., un poco animato

più lento

rit.

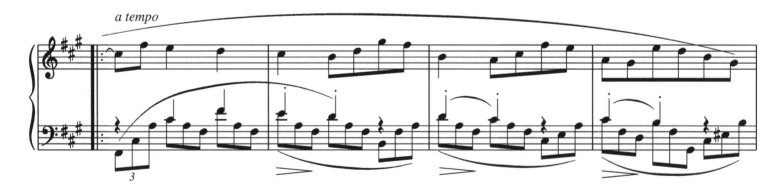

a tempo

rit.

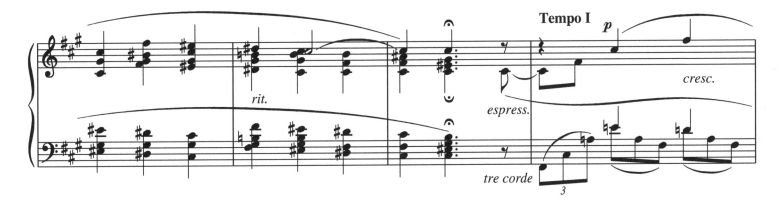

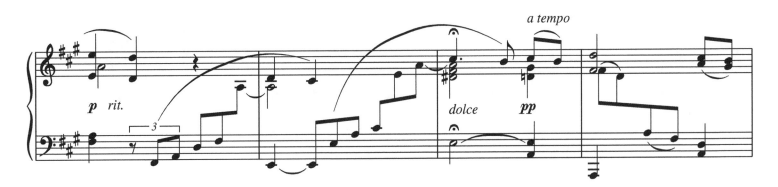

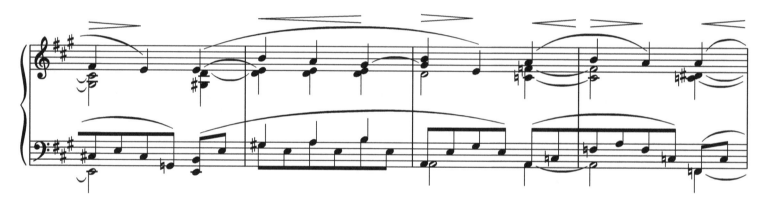

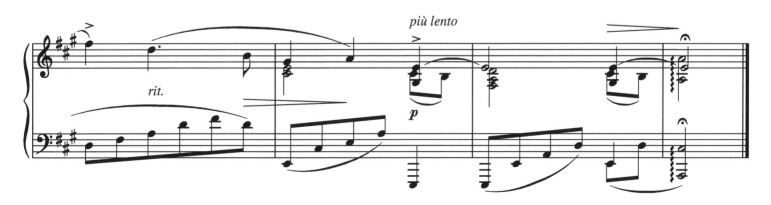

Jupiter

"The Bringer of Jollity," Chorale Theme
from the symphonic cycle THE PLANETS

Gustav Holst
1874–1934
Op. 32
originally for orchestra

La fille aux cheveux de lin

(The Girl with the Flaxen Hair)

Claude Debussy
1862–1918

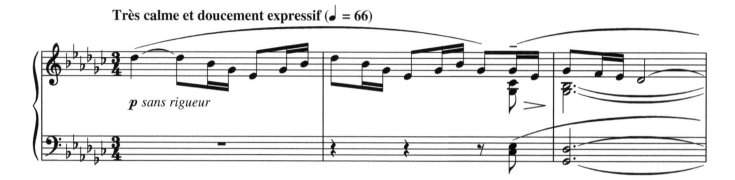

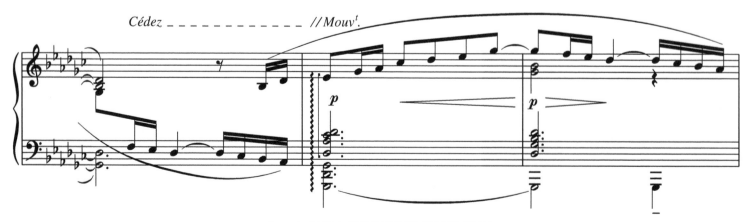

Laudate Dominum

from VESPERAE SOLENNES DE CONFESSORE

Wolfgang Amadeus Mozart
1756–1791
K 339
originally for soprano, orchestra and chorus

Andante ma un poco sostenuto

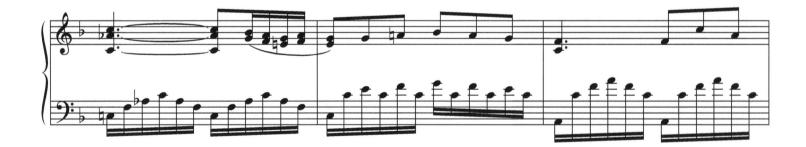

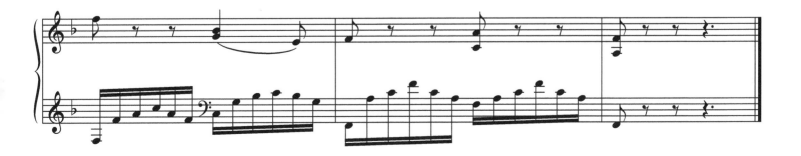

Largo

"Ombra mai fù" from the opera SERSE

George Frideric Handel
1685–1759

Mandolin Concerto in C Major
First Movement Excerpt

Antonio Vivaldi
1678–1741
originally for mandolin and orchestra

Meditation
from the opera THAÏS

Jules Massenet
1842–1912

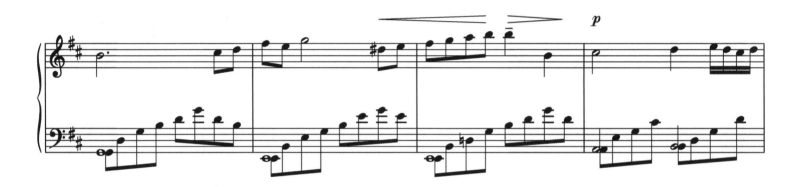

To Coda ⊕ **A Tempo più mosso** ♩ = 69

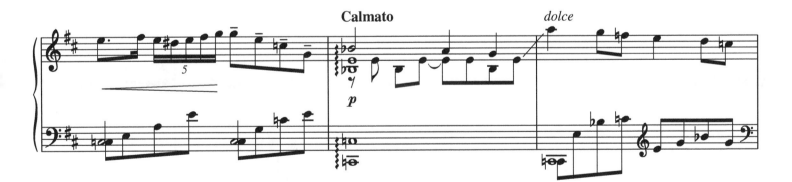

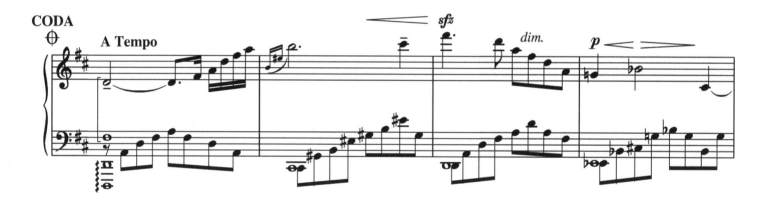

My Heart Ever Faithful

from CANTATA 68

Johann Sebastian Bach
1685–1750

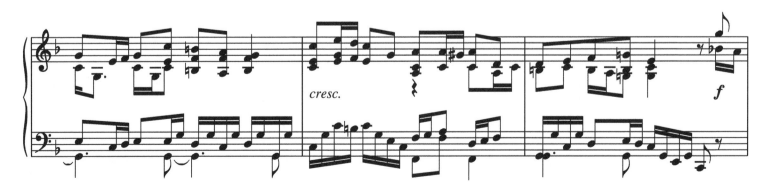

Minuet
from PARTITA NO. 1

Johann Sebastian Bach
1685–1750

[Allegretto]

[mf]

1.

2.

Nimrod
from ENIGMA VARIATIONS

Edward Elgar
1857–1934
Op. 36
originally for orchestra

O mio babbino caro
from the opera GIANNI SCHICCHI

Giacomo Puccini
1858–1924

Andante ingenuo ♪ = 120

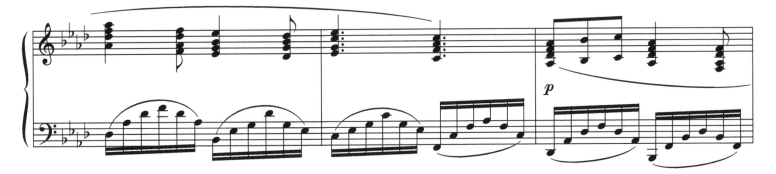

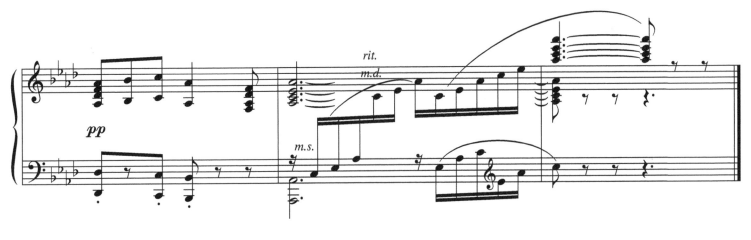

Ode to Joy
from SYMPHONY NO. 9 IN D MINOR

Ludwig van Beethoven
1770–1827

Panis angelicus

César Franck
1822–1890
originally for tenor and
instrumental ensemble

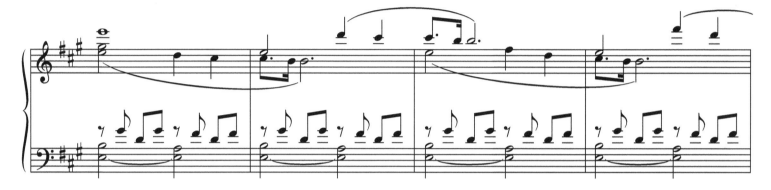

Piano Concerto No. 21 in C Major

"Elvira Madigan"
Second Movement Excerpt

Wolfgang Amadeus Mozart
1756–1791
K 467
originally for piano and orchestra

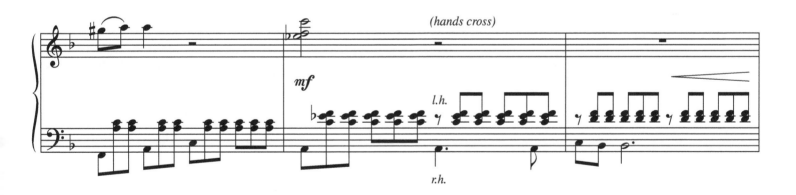

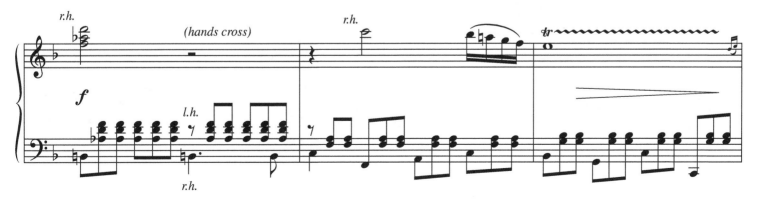

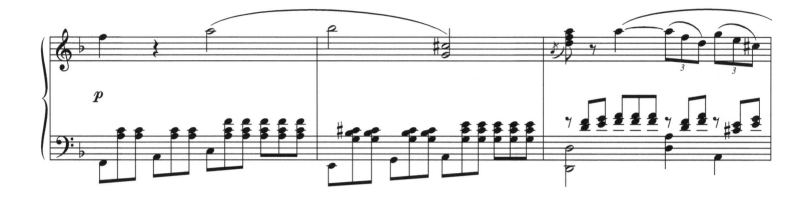

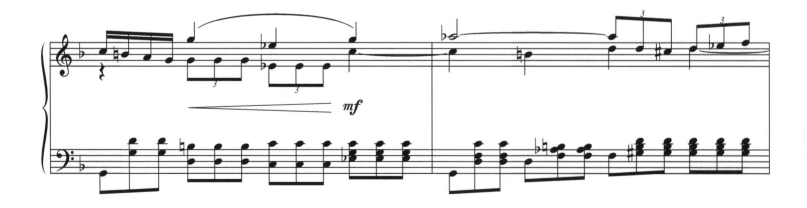

Prelude in C Major
from THE WELL-TEMPERED CLAVIER, BOOK 1

Johann Sebastian Bach
1685–1750

[rit.]

Rêverie

Claude Debussy
1862–1918

Andante sans lenteur (not too slowly)

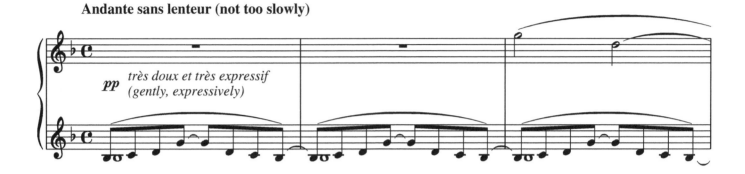

_pp_ _très doux et très expressif_
(gently, expressively)

meno **p**

_mf_

dim.

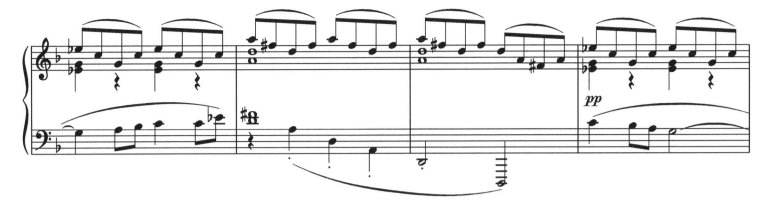

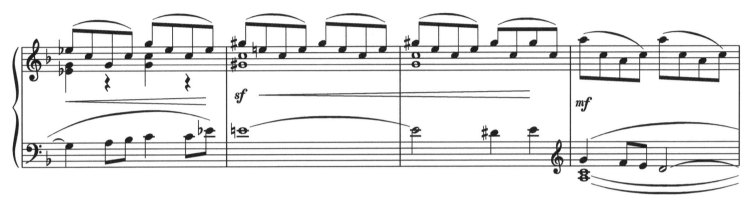

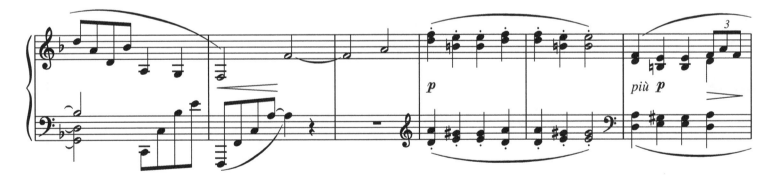

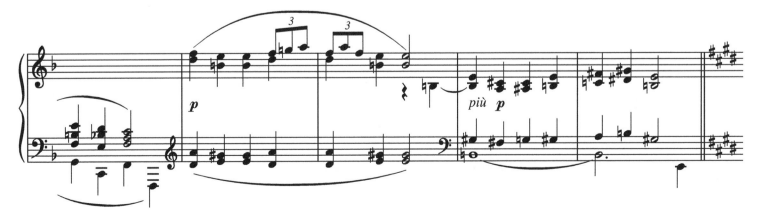

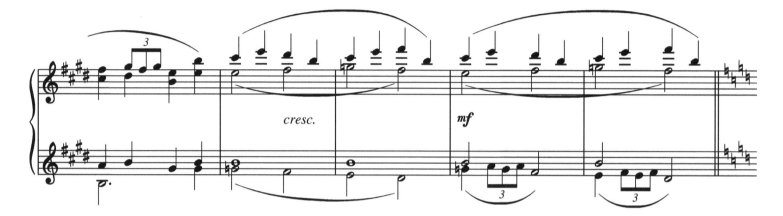

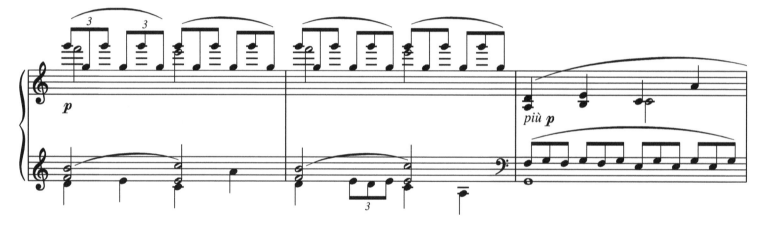

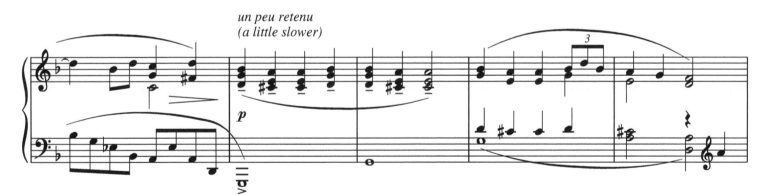

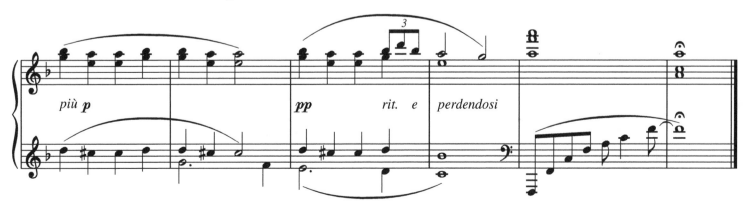

Rhapsody on a Theme of Paganini
Variation XVIII

Sergei Rachmaninoff
1873–1943
Op. 43
originally for piano and orchestra

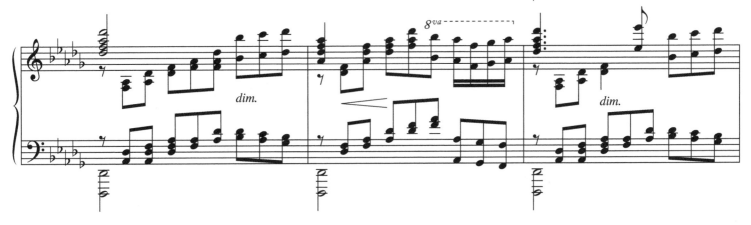

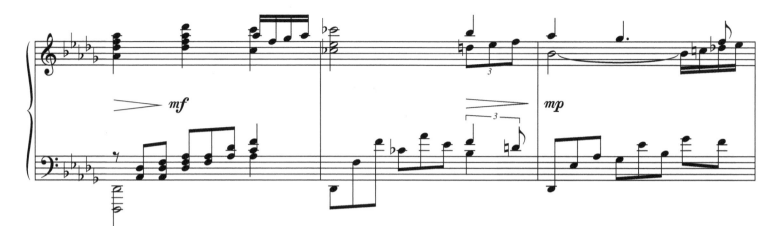

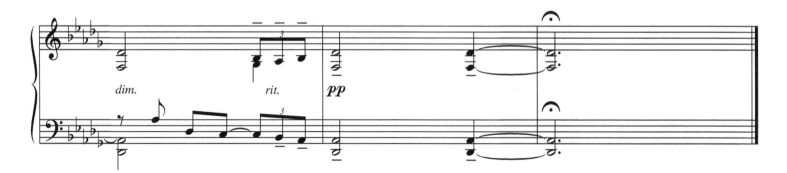

Spring

from THE FOUR SEASONS
First Movement Excerpt

Antonio Vivaldi
1678-1741
RV269, P241, M76, Op. 8, No. 1
originally for violin & string orchestra

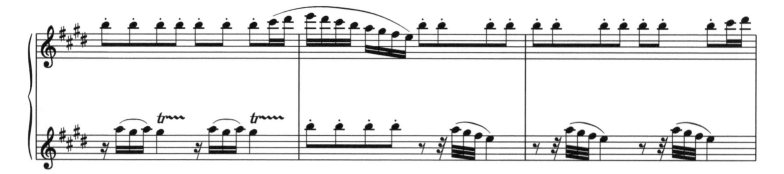

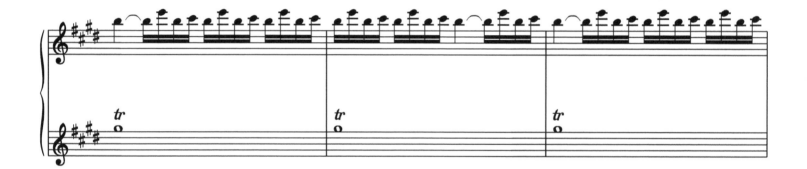

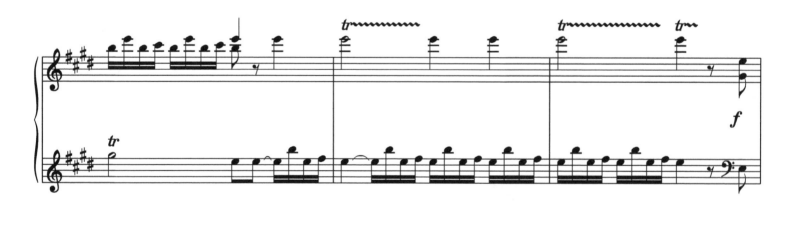

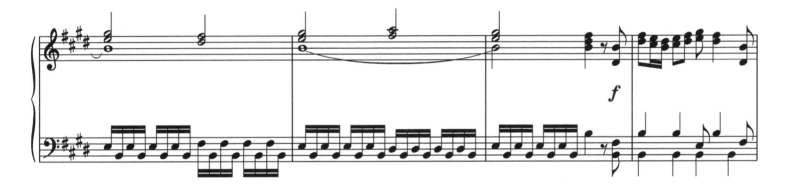

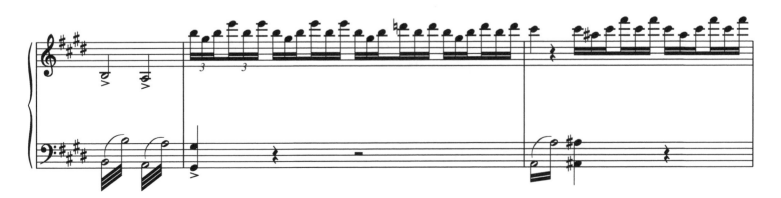

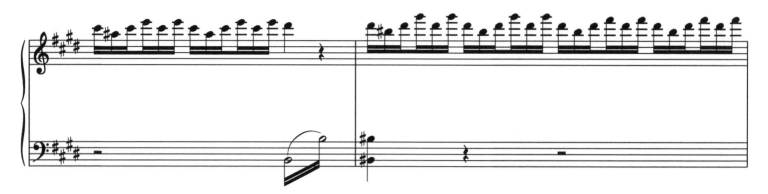

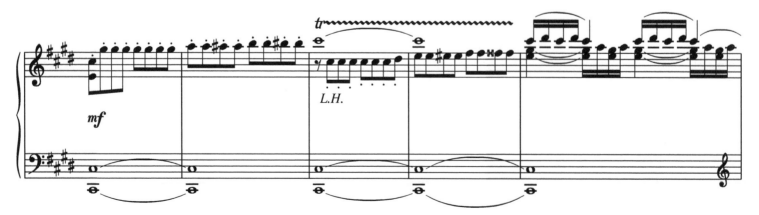

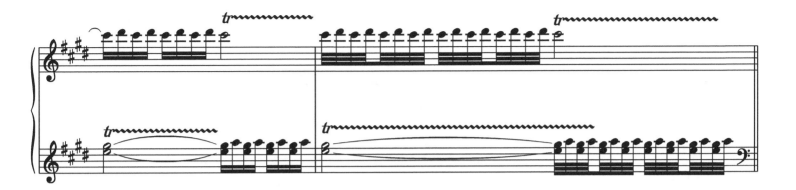

Rondeau

Excerpt

Jean-Joseph Mouret
1682–1738

Sheep may safely graze

from Cantata 208 ("Birthday Cantata")

Johann Sebastian Bach
1685–1750
BWV 208
originally for soprano,
2 flutes and continuo

Symphony No. 9 in E Minor

"From the New World"
Second Movement Excerpt ("Largo")

Antonín Dvořák
1841–1904
Op. 95
originally for orchestra

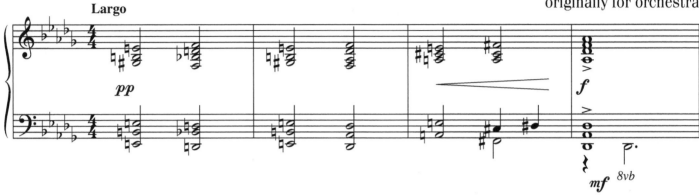

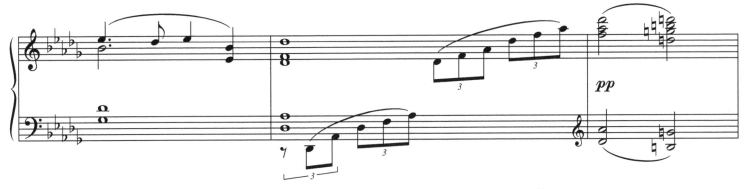

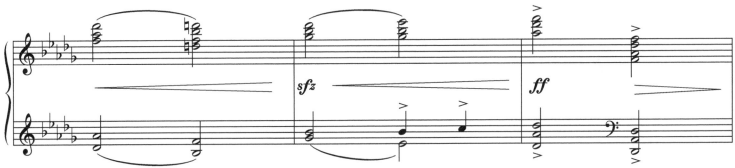

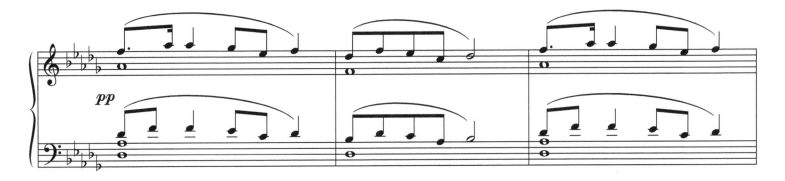

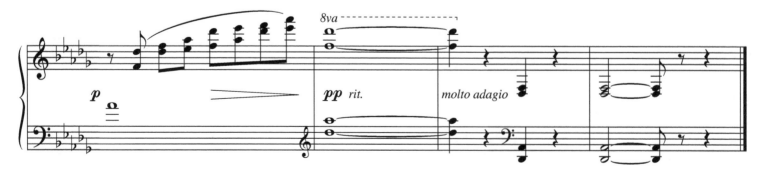

Trumpet Voluntary

Jeremiah Clarke
1670–1707

Andante con moto

Trumpet Tune

Henry Purcell
1659–1695

Wedding March
from A MIDSUMMER NIGHT'S DREAM

Felix Mendelssohn
1809–1847

Allegro

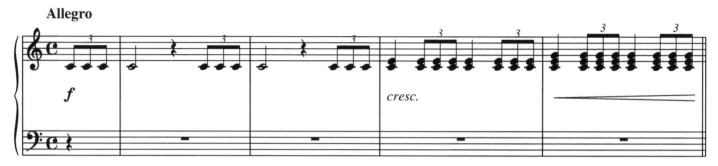

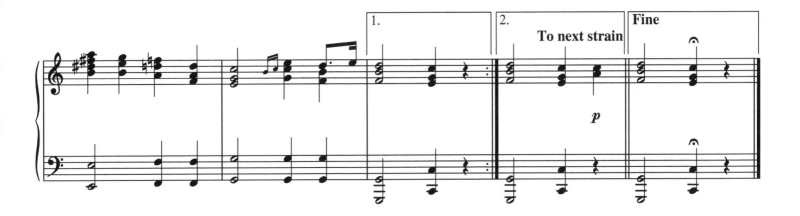

D.S. al Fine

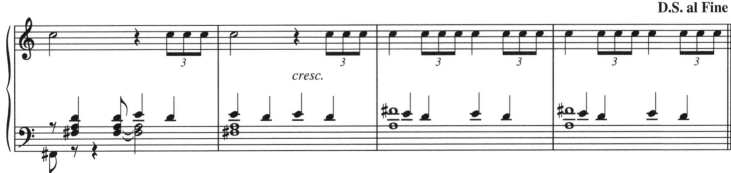

Widmung
(Dedication)

Robert Schumann
1810–1856
Op. 25, No. 1
originally for voice and piano

Innig, lebhaft

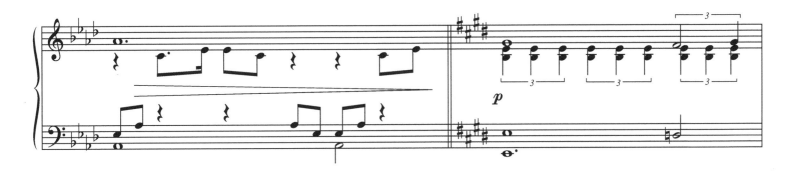

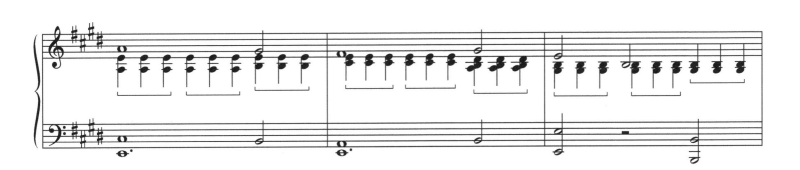

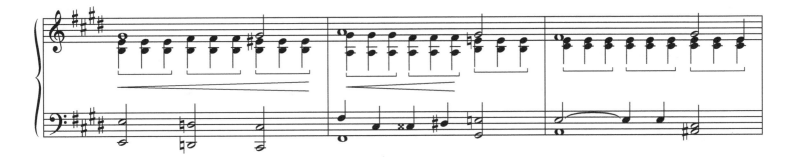

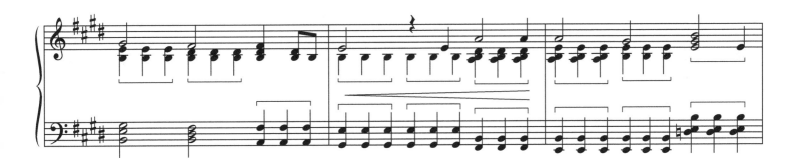

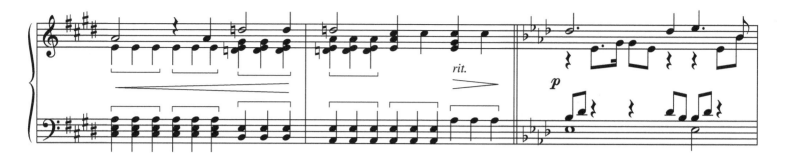

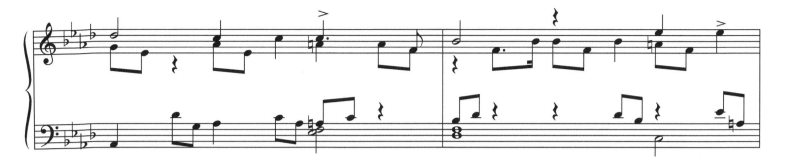

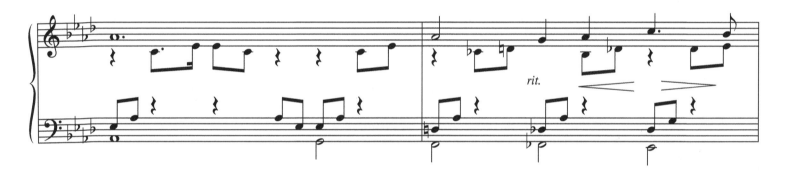

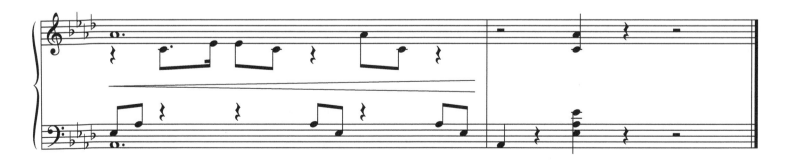

World's Great Classical Music

This ambitious series is comprised entirely of new editions of some of the world's most beloved classical music. Each volume includes dozens of selections by the major talents in the history of European art music: Bach, Beethoven, Berlioz, Brahms, Debussy, Dvořák, Handel, Haydn, Mahler, Mendelssohn, Mozart, Rachmaninoff, Schubert, Schumann, Tchaikovsky, Verdi, Vivaldi, and dozens of other composers.

Easy to Intermediate Piano

The Baroque Era
00240057 Piano Solo $17.99

Beethoven
00220034 Piano Solo $15.99

The Classical Era
00240061 Piano Solo $15.99

Classical Masterpieces
00290520 Piano Solo $19.99

Easier Piano Classics
00290519 Piano Solo $16.99

Favorite Classical Themes
00220021 Piano Solo $18.99

Great Easier Piano Literature
00310304 Piano Solo $16.99

Mozart – Simplified Piano Solos
00220028 Piano Solo $16.99

Opera's Greatest Melodies
00220023 Piano Solo $18.99

The Romantic Era
00240068 Piano Solo $16.99

The Symphony
00220041 Piano Solo $14.95

Tchaikovsky – Simplified Piano Solos
00220027 Piano Solo $15.99

Intermediate to Advanced Piano

Bach
00220037 Piano Solo $16.99

The Baroque Era
00240060 Piano Solo $16.99

Beethoven
00220033 Piano Solo $15.95

Chopin Piano Music
00240344 Piano Solo $16.99

The Classical Era
00240063 Piano Solo $17.99

Debussy Piano Music
00240343 Piano Solo $17.99

Great Classical Themes
00310300 Piano Solo $15.99

Great Piano Literature
00310302 Piano Solo $18.99

Mozart
00220025 Piano Solo $14.99

Opera at the Piano
00310297 Piano Solo $16.99

Piano Classics
00290518 Piano Solo $17.99

Piano Preludes
00240248 Piano Solo $18.99

The Romantic Era
00240096 Piano Solo $16.99

Johann Strauss
00220035 Piano Solo $14.95

The Symphony
00220032 Piano Solo $16.99

Tchaikovsky
00220026 Piano Solo $15.99

Instrumental

The Baroque and Classical Flute
00841550 Flute and Piano $19.99

Masterworks for Guitar
00699503 Classical Guitar.................. $16.95

The Romantic Flute
00240210 Flute and Piano $17.99

Vocal

Gilbert & Sullivan
00740142 Piano/Vocal...................... $22.99

HAL•LEONARD®

www.halleonard.com

Prices, content and availability subject to change without notice.

0217